# The C Class Advantage

# Benefits for the Contrarian Real Estate Investor

by
Jayson Morris

© **Copyright 2017 - All rights reserved.**

Except as permitted as under the U.S. Copyright Act of 1976, no part of this book may be copied, stored, reproduced, republished, uploaded, posted, transmitted, altered or distributed in any way, in whole or part in any form or any medium, or incorporated into any other work, without the express prior written permission except in the case of brief quotations embodied in critical reviews or articles.

Your support of the author's rights is appreciated.

The scanning, uploading and distribution of this book via the Internet or via any other means without the permission of the publisher is illegal and punishable by law. Please purchase only authorized editions, and do not participate in or encourage electronic piracy of copyrighted materials.

Disclaimers:

The information provided within this book is for general informational purposes only. While we try to keep the information up-to-date and correct, there are no representations or warranties, express or implied, about the completeness, accuracy, reliability, suitability or availability with respect to the information, products, services, or related graphics contained in this book for any purpose. Any use of this information is at your own risk.

The author and publisher have made every effort to ensure the accuracy of the information within this book was correct at time of publication. The author and publisher do not assume and hereby disclaim any liability to any party for any loss, damage, or disruption caused by errors or omissions, whether such errors or omissions result from accident, negligence, or any other cause.

Readers acknowledge that the author is not engaging in the rendering of legal, financial, medical or professional advice. The content of this book has been derived from various sources. Please consult a licensed professional before attempting any techniques outlined in this book.

Under no circumstances will any legal responsibility or blame be held against the publisher for any reparation, damages, or monetary loss due to the information herein, either directly or indirectly.

Trademarks are used without permission. Use of the trademark is not authorized by, associated with, or sponsored by the trademark owners. All trademarks and brands used within this book are used with no intent to infringe on the trademark owners and are only used for clarification purposes.

By reading this document, the reader agrees that under no circumstances is the author and publisher responsible for any losses, direct or indirect, which are incurred as a result of the use of information contained within this document, including, but not limited to, —errors, omissions, or inaccuracies.

# Table of Contents

Introduction .................................................................. 1

Chapter 1: Classes of Real Estate Property ............ 4

Chapter 2: Class C Rental Properties .................... 12

Chapter 3: Misconceptions about Class C Properties .............................................................. 24

Chapter 4: Affordability of Class C Properties .... 33

Chapter 5: Return on Investment for Class C Properties .............................................................. 42

Chapter 6: The Risks of Class C Properties ......... 53

Chapter 7: Swimming Against the Current ......... 59

Conclusion ............................................................. 65

# Introduction

Most people dream of investing in real estate in some way. You can do this either as a homeowner or a landlord. However, many do not clearly understand what it takes to become a successful real estate investor. Before you take that first step to investing in real estate, it is important that you understand the different classes of properties that are usually available on the market. Most real estate professionals categorize properties into four distinct classes – A, B, C, and D.

In this book, I offer an in-depth guide to investing in C class properties. I go ahead and talk about the other three classes of properties in the first chapter, but the primary focus of this book will be class C real estate properties and their unique characteristics.

The book covers a brief description of the different classes of real estate and what separates them from each other. It is important to learn to identify the type of property you are dealing with every time you want to make an investment in real estate.

I also provide a detailed analysis of C class rentals, especially in the Midwestern region of the United States. We all know that the Midwest has been facing some serious challenges compared to the rest of the United States when it comes to the property market. I discuss the diverse purchase price points of different states and cities in the Midwest. I also offer an analysis of the rent rates within this region. Of course, as an investor, you would be interested in knowing the type of neighborhood that a typical C class rental would be located, as well as the demographic that inhabits these areas. This is covered in the book as well.

If you aren't a keen real estate investor, you are likely to believe the many myths and misconceptions about investing in C class properties. Many investors shy away from buying properties in C class communities, but this book clarifies some of these misconceptions and reveals the truth about how lucrative this segment of the market can be.

C class properties can bring in a massive return on investment if you happen to have the right information. There are numerous benefits to purchasing and renting out C class properties as long as you understand how to go about it. Obviously, there are also some risks that come with investing in C class real estate, but all investments carry some element of risk. We try to highlight some of the potential dangers so that you don't end up jumping into these kinds of properties with your eyes closed.

The truth is that investing requires knowledge and skill. Most so called real estate investors don't really bother analyzing the market conditions for themselves. They simply believe what others are saying and follow the crowd, but you won't make money that way. With the help of this book, you will be able to do your own due diligence and avoid following the herd. In most cases, going against the grain will have you end up making a wiser decision.

It is my hope that by the time you finish reading this book, you will have the crucial information required to start looking at C class real estate as a **seriously** viable investment.

Enjoy the book!

# Chapter 1: Classes of Real Estate Property

Why is it important to classify properties?

First of all, real estate brokers, lenders, and investors have created these classifications in order to make communication easier amongst themselves when it comes to the rating and quality of properties.

If you are a property investor, one of the reasons why you must understand these classifications is so that you are able to determine the return on investment and risk level to expect. This is very important if you want to become a successful and strategic real estate investor. Most of the people who invest in real estate often rely on their emotions too much and simply look at the physical aspects of a property. Yet the secret to being a successful real estate investor lies in focusing on how each property fits into your objectives and the level of risk you are willing to accept.

Properties are also classified so that you can be able to identify the type of tenants or homeowners you will be dealing with. This helps you determine how to market your property to people who are looking for houses or apartments to rent. You will be in a stronger position to gauge the competitive position of a property within the market in relation to its value and rental rates.

The different classifications highlight different returns and risks because the grading is done according to the location of the property and its physical characteristics. In this chapter, we are going to classify properties into the same four groups that most American property investors use. These are Class A, B, C, and D.

## *Class A Properties*

This is considered as the top tier in a real estate market. These types of properties are generally of a high-end architectural design and construction, for example, luxury condos. They incorporate a lot of state-of-the-art technology and mechanical systems, as well as an assortment of real estate amenities.

The property is likely to have granite countertops and hardwood floors, which are just some of the features that are in-demand. Class A properties may include superior services like valet parking, locker room facilities, on-site coffee bars, and restaurant facilities. They may provide settings and services that are resort-like, such as fountains and lavish fitness centers.

In terms of location, Class A properties are generally found in suburban neighborhoods or gated communities. They command very high rent rates. These areas have new buildings which are usually less than 10 years old. This means that you will not have too many maintenance issues to deal with. These areas also have some of the best private and public schools.

As an investor, buying property in a Class A location means you will be targeting wealthy and high-quality tenants, so you will not have to deal with high vacancy rates. The demographic for Class A tenants include business owners, mid-level managers, and white collar workers.

The flip side of Class A real estate is that they do not generate a high amount of cash flow. This is primarily because of their high demand as an "easy" investment. You should invest in Class A properties if you want to get returns from the appreciation of the real estate. However, be forewarned, appreciation is never guaranteed.

## *Class B Properties*

This class is probably the most common group of properties and includes well-maintained duplexes or multi-family buildings as well as single family homes in nice neighborhoods. These properties are slightly less luxurious compared to those in

Class A in terms of the quality, location, and amenities provided.

Investors may choose to buy a Class B property as an asset, but in most cases, such properties result from the aging of Class A buildings. These properties are generally between 15 to 30 years old.

Class B properties tend to be in good condition and attract rent rates that are considered above average. In some cases, a property may have assets that are well-maintained yet still be graded as Class B simply because they have structures that are technically outdated. A good example would be a house with single pane windows and low ceilings or a building with small elevator cabs.

Such properties are considered by investors to be "value-add" opportunities since you can renovate and upgrade them back up to a Class A property. Investors looking to buy Class B properties have to do so at a higher CAP rate because of the higher risk compared to Class A properties.

Class B properties are located in decent, middle-class areas that have good schools and restaurants. Tenants are mostly young adults or entry-level managers. If you are investing in a retail shopping center, you must also bear the fact that the quality of the tenants can influence the classification of the whole property. Rent rates will obviously be much lower than Class A and you may have to deal with higher maintenance costs due to the aging of the property.

## *Class C Properties*

These are low rated properties that are only surpassed in undesirability by Class D properties. The spaces are barely functional and the rent is cheap. Most Class C properties tend to be old and outdated assets that are in dire need of renovations and maintenance. The plumbing and electrical systems are likely to be falling apart and the finishing needs work.

They are located in lower-income areas where buildings are generally more than 30 years old. The demographic of the tenants are blue collar and hourly employees who may only have a high school diploma. Some of the tenants may be relying on government subsidies or working for low wages. The business environment may include a lot of pawn shops and check-cashing businesses.

## *Class D Properties*

These kinds of buildings tend to be on their last legs and are creeping toward functional obsolescence. Such properties usually have boarded-up windows and appear to be vacant. They may bear some similarities to Class C properties except they are in a state of much greater neglect.

As an investor, prepare to walk into a building that is virtually uninhabitable and in dire need of major repairs. The tenants that are likely to be attracted to such properties tend to be very low-income workers who live below the poverty line. The location resembles a war zone and you would not want to be walking through these areas alone. This is due to the high level of crime and drug peddling that sometimes have the cops running scared.

The great thing about these properties is that you can buy them dirt cheap. On the other hand, if you are a serious investor looking for real estate to buy and rent out, we recommend that you avoid this class of properties. Of course, you can still go ahead if you know what you are doing, but otherwise, Class D properties should be left to slumlords.

## *Factors Affecting Classification*

It is important to note that these classifications are not rigidly defined. They are merely indications to help you get a general idea of the different classes of properties that you can invest in. In fact, real estate properties can move either up or down in classification.

For example, a building may be newly constructed and be classified as Class A. As time passes and it ages, tenants change, or the type of businesses in the area shift, it could slowly be downgraded to a Class B. You should also realize just how critical the type of business being conducted in the property is. If you are investing in a retail center, then you must consider the location of the relevant infrastructure. If the traffic patterns change toward new areas, the previously Class A property may find itself within a Class C zone.

The reverse is also true, and this is where savvy value-add investors come in. A Class C property can be renovated and the tenants repositioned in order to elevate its status. As cash flow improves, the value and classification of the property may also go up.

One of the fundamental questions you must ask yourself at this point is this: Does the property class correlate to the expected returns? The truth is that, in the majority of cases, there is little correlation between the two. In the instances where a correlation does exist, it is usually inversely related. In other words, if you compare Class A, B, and C properties and their potential returns, an investor would make the most money buying and renting out Class C real estate. Class C acquisitions tend to generate greater cash flow over time compared to the other two categories.

What is important to understand is that each of these classes has their own benefits and disadvantages. The top-tier properties may cost you more in terms of the purchase price but you will have fewer migraines when it comes to maintenance and tenants. At the bottom end, you will generate more of a regular income in the long term as long as you have a sound business strategy.

The best advice, as always, is to examine your investing strategy and decide which class of properties works best for you. Put every investment opportunity within the right context with regard to potential returns and risks. As long as you can validate that the targeted real estate you want to acquire is competitive in its property class and will remain so for many years to come, you would be headed in the right direction.

# Chapter 2: Class C Rental Properties

We have already highlighted some of the significant characteristics that define your average Class C property. As an investor, you should know that this class of real estate is a great way to generate cash flow. Once you acquire such a property and renovate it, you can rent out space to tenants and receive a regular income for a long time.

In this chapter, we are going to dive into a detailed analysis of Class C rentals. We shall examine the general purchase prices of Class C properties in the Midwestern region of the United States, as well as their typical rental rates. We will also describe what a general Class C neighborhood looks like and the type of tenants that you may potentially come across.

## *Purchase Price Points for Class C Properties*

According to the National Association of Realtors, the Midwest experienced a 5.7% rise in the average price of homes in the final quarter of 2016. By the end of the year 2016, the median price was about $181,000 all across the Midwest.

Here is the detailed current data regarding each state in the region and the typical purchase price points for multi-family rental units.

### 1. Illinois

The median value for Class C properties is $84,200.

### 2. Indiana

The median value for Class C properties is $64,700.

### 3. Iowa

The median value for Class C properties is $82,000.

### 4. Kansas

The median value for Class C properties is $61,800.

## 5. Michigan

The median value for Class C properties is $64,200.

## 6. Minnesota

The median value for Class C properties is $124,000.

## 7. Missouri

The median value for Class C properties is $74,100.

## 8. Nebraska

The median value for Class C properties is $85,600.

## 9. North Dakota

The median value for Class C properties is $126,000.

### 10. Ohio

The median value for Class C properties is $68,100.

### 11. South Dakota

The median value for Class C properties is $120,000.

### 12. Wisconsin

The median value for Class C properties is $104,000.

## *Rent Rates for Class C Properties*

The following statistics are attributed to data collected by the Census ACS survey of 2015. Median and mean rent data for 2016 is scheduled to be released in September of 2017.

We are going to cover the median and average residential rental rates in the Midwest on a state by state basis. These are rental statistics representing monthly rates. It is important to note that the median rent is a more precise depiction of Class C property rental rates. It refers to the middle of the rent distribution and is generally preferred when analyzing such data.

### 1. Illinois

The median gross residential rent paid by tenants was $936. The average gross rent was $988. These are the highest rates experienced in the state since 2005.

### 2. Indiana

The median gross residential rent paid by tenants was $758. The average gross rent was $760. These are the highest rates experienced in the state since 2005.

### 3. Iowa

The median gross residential rent paid by tenants was $718. The average gross rent was $729. These are the highest rates experienced in the state since 2005.

### 4. Kansas

The median gross residential rent paid by tenants was $803. The average gross rent was $816. These

are the highest rates experienced in the state since 2005.

## 5. Michigan

The median gross residential rent paid by tenants was $718. The average gross rent was $729. These are the highest rates experienced in the state since 2005.

## 6. Minnesota

The median gross residential rent paid by tenants was $888. The average gross rent was $916. These are the highest rates experienced in the state since 2005.

## 7. Missouri

The median gross residential rent paid by tenants was $763. The average gross rent was $772. These are the highest rates experienced in the state since 2005.

## 8. Nebraska

The median gross residential rent paid by tenants was $750. The average gross rent was $768. These

are the highest rates experienced in the state since 2005.

### 9. North Dakota

The median gross residential rent paid by tenants was $775. The average gross rent was $816. These are the highest rates experienced in the state since 2005.

### 10.     Ohio

The median gross residential rent paid by tenants was $746. The average gross rent was $756. These are the highest rates experienced in the state since 2005.

### 11. South Dakota

The median gross residential rent paid by tenants was $675. The average gross rent was $675. These are the highest rates experienced in the state since 2005.

### 12. Wisconsin

The median gross residential rent paid by tenants was $792. The average gross rent was $807. These

are the highest rates experienced in the state since 2005.

## *Class C Neighborhoods*

As an investor looking to build substantial passive income and generate wealth through rental properties, it would be a great idea to acquire Class C properties. These properties are usually located in specific types of neighborhoods, and it is crucial that you get a clear picture of what these areas are like before you decide what kind of investments to make.

Class C neighborhoods have substantial amenities and anchors, for example, churches, schools, and strip malls. The schools are usually run down and have few amenities. The students are primarily from low-income families. The churches in these areas are generally small and tend to be very family-oriented since people know each other well. The malls are nothing like the major retail establishments you would find in large cities. They are just long, one-story buildings with narrow parking at the front.

The ratio of tenants to homeowners can be as high as 50%, and in some cases much higher. These neighborhoods are located in some of the lowest priced sections of the city or state. The ratio of rent to property value is very high, sometimes more than 2%. This is why Class C areas tend to have the highest CAP rates and cash-on-cash returns in relation to the other property classes.

In other words, these are the neighborhoods that most landlords make the most money from. These Class C properties tend to be very cheap to acquire as an investment and are typically owned by private investment groups and private investors. If you refer to the purchase prices of single family homes in the section above, you will see that these neighborhoods have very affordable homes.

## *Dealing With Class C Tenants*

Class C neighborhoods are usually low-income areas that are inhabited by people who earn low wages. Some of the residents of Class C areas are on government assistance. The majority of tenants in such areas cannot qualify to live in better environments, and this means that landlords are likely to charge them a premium. As an investor, you buy the property at an affordable price and with charge market-level rents, thus ending up with a handsome profit.

Since you will be dealing with low-income tenants, you will find yourself constantly enduring numerous evictions due to unpaid rents. The tenants in Class C neighborhoods are also extremely vocal in complaining about housing conditions. They know that they can't afford to move elsewhere, so they don't have a choice but to complain.

Most of the tenants in these areas also have a penchant for lying to the property managers in order to get housing. For example, many will not hesitate to give fake references or fake rental histories. In some cases, a tenant may be undergoing eviction from one building and at the same time, they are applying for another apartment.

Dealing with Class C tenants can be a hassle, so you had better be prepared to tough it out. One of the best ways of handling these issues would be to hire a competent property manager who has enough experience dealing with such tenants. At the end of the day, however, the money you make will make up for the stress of dealing with your tenants.

## Finding the right tenants

Just because you are investing in Class C rental properties does not mean you automatically have to put up with Class C tenants. There are things that you can do to actually improve the chances of getting good tenants who pay their rent on time, have good credit scores, and won't mess up your property. Of course, this becomes difficult if your property is an old apartment or home next to a mini-mart. However, it is still possible to find and keep high-class tenants in a Class C building.

Here are a few recommendations:

1. Advertise the criteria you will use to screen applicants. When placing your vacancy ad, list down specific criteria such as mandatory criminal background checks, income to rent ratio, rental history checks, and minimum credit score. You can also state the cost of screening applicants. This will go a long way in weeding out potentially problematic tenants who will simply look for landlords who have lower standards.

2. Clean your units well. Make sure that your building or property is well maintained if you want to attract decent tenants. This may require a significant investment but you have to do it if you genuinely want good prospective clients. Avoid showing the property if the place is full of cobwebs or the carpets are filthy. Though you may promise a potential tenant that the place will be tidied before they move in, they may decide to pass up the opportunity and go elsewhere. In case the unit being advertised still has a tenant, you could find a way of incentivizing them to keep the place clean during the scheduled showings.

3. Ensure that all the necessary repairs are done, especially those that may be violating county or city housing codes. As an investor, you do not want to give your property manager or landlord a bad name by refusing to buy a new flush valve or fix a leaking roof. Decent tenants will not tolerate living under such conditions and will simply choose not to renew their leases. Coincidentally, having your building in a state of disrepair attracts shady tenants who are looking for housing where nobody seems to care about the rules. These kinds of tenants won't bother reporting you to the housing authorities but they will also contribute to the damage of your property.

4. Read keenly through tenant's credit reports. It is possible that you may come across a Class A tenant who is going through some tough financial challenges. This may have resulted in a reduced credit score. You will have to check their credit report keenly to see the pattern of their payments, for example, repayment of credit card debt, car payments, utilities, employment history, and debt-to-income ratio. These will help you determine whether the tenant is worth the risk, despite their recent financial hurdles.

# Chapter 3: Misconceptions about Class C Properties

Most people who invest in Class C properties usually go into the community with prior misconceptions about the type of people they will be dealing with. Class C properties tend to be old, run down, and are located in crime prone areas. Therefore, it is easy to make a quick conclusion that the surrounding community is a reflection of what the property looks like.

When some investors think of Class C properties, they visualize ghettos, slums, hordes of unemployed or low-wage workers, dysfunctional families, and substance abuse. Not all real estate investors have this view, but the majority tends to believe these myths.

In this chapter, we are going to look into some of the common misconceptions of Class C communities. As an investor, you want to make investment decisions based on facts. Class C properties have a huge potential to make you a lot of money in the long term if you play your cards right. There is no reason to fear Class C tenants, and as you are about to learn, in most cases the problem isn't with the tenants at all.

## *Misconception 1: All Class C Tenants are Troublemakers*

This misconception is based on the assumption that all low-income earners, who are the primary occupants of Class C rental properties, are rowdy and undisciplined. This is a total fallacy because anyone, regardless of economic status, can behave badly.

There are some investors who have bought Class A and B rental properties in really nice neighborhoods but ended up with tenants who can only be considered monsters. Perceptions can oftentimes be misleading. A young upcoming businessman driving a sleek Jaguar may seem like a great tenant, thus prompting you to skip the screening process altogether. It is only after they have moved in that you realize just how much damage they can do to your property.

Now, while it is true that there are many bad tenants who live in Class C buildings, it would be wrong to lump them all into the same category. In fact, the majority of tenants tend to follow the rules set by the property manager and try to be cooperative at all times.

If you consider the demographic that tends to occupy Class C properties, you would expect to come across many who are high school graduates working blue collar jobs. The jobs may not be paying much but these are hardworking people who are just trying to get by. The majority of them may even turn out to be lifelong renters, which is a great thing for any real estate investor. Many Class C tenants will only consider a move if they find a better or cheaper place, or if they are dealing with a bad landlord. Keep in mind that these tenants have families, and once the kids become attached to their friends in the nearby school, moving out becomes difficult. At the end of the day, as long as your rental units are constantly occupied, you continue to enjoy a healthy cash flow.

Of course, there are going to be some bad apples within the bunch but it is the responsibility of the property manager to make sure that all tenants are thoroughly vetted prior to being allocated housing. Your first line of defense should be the screening of all applicants. This may take some time, which is why almost half of all landlords choose not to check their potential tenants for criminal backgrounds or even contact previous landlords. This small step may seem tedious but it is definitely worth it. In the event that you do end up with some bad tenants once they have moved in, there are always legal courses of action that you can take.

## *Misconception 2: Class C Tenants are Destructive*

Many investors fear taking up Class C properties because they do not want to deal with tenants who are considered destructive. This is based on the misconception that those tenants who occupy Class C units willingly and maliciously destroy the owner's property. This is simply untrue.

As we said before, the tendency to destroy property is not the preserve of low-income tenants. There are cases where tenants in high-end properties throw large and extravagant parties and end up destroying the place. The apartment ends up with damaged walls and buckled wood flooring due to water exposure. Some are so cocky that they even file restraining orders against the landlords when complaints are made against them. Needless to say, they leave the owner with thousands of dollars in repair costs. It is clear to see that destructive tenants are not just limited to Class C properties.

This is not to say that there won't be destructive tenants in Class C areas. However, making the decision not to invest in a Class property would be foolish, especially if it is based on a wrong assumption like fear of destructive tenants. Anyone can trash your property if given the chance, regardless of their level of income. This is why you have to go the extra mile to check out potential occupants when they apply.

What you need to keep in mind at all times is that background checks are important, and if you can contact past landlords, then do it. It is recommended that you talk to at least two or three previous landlords because the current one may lie just to get rid of a problematic tenant. A tenant who is in the habit of destroying property will likely have a record of evictions, legal, or criminal incidents. These are things that reveal the true behavior of a person. If you are still worried about property destruction, then interview the prospective tenants in person. Listen to the kind of complaints they are making about their previous landlords. If they complain too much, then you are likely to become their next victim.

The bottom line is, if you do not do your due diligence in screening prospective tenants of your rental units, you will likely end up with some knuckleheads who won't mind trashing the place.

## *Misconception 3: Class C Properties are Located in War Zones*

When it comes to investing in Class C properties, you are likely to end up buying real estate located in low-income neighborhoods. The problem that most investors have is they believe that these neighborhoods are active war zones where gangs of thugs roam the streets, randomly shooting into buildings. This misconception has led many an investor to pass up an awesome opportunity to generate a healthy cash flow.

The truth is that low-income areas tend to suffer greater levels of crime than the high or middle-class areas. That is a fact. But this does not mean that these places are war zones and are therefore uninhabitable. This is a gross generalization that is usually perpetuated by those who have never lived in urban or inner city areas. What you see on the news is rarely the actual situation on the ground. By the way, you do not want to be the kind of real estate investor who makes business decisions based on negative reporting on TV.

As an investor, your primary concern with this kind of situation would be the lack of decent, law-abiding tenants for your rental units. The fear is based on having your property unoccupied for long periods of time, or in extreme cases, occupied by criminals who may not enjoy paying your rent at all. Unlike the previous two misconceptions that dealt with undesirable tenants, this is one false impression that cannot be resolved by screening applicants. So what do you do?

Whenever you are thinking of acquiring investment properties in Class C areas, the smart thing to do is to first understand the neighborhood. Not all Class C neighborhoods are created equal. There are different levels of crime and diverse groups of people living in those areas. You may find some real estate in a blighted and crime-prone area, or you can discover great properties in the upper levels of a low-income neighborhood. Regardless of the generalizations that people make, there are always great investment opportunities even in low-income areas.

You have to be keen and study the area well. If you want to get a good return on your investment, you should consider buying properties located next to social amenities, such as schools, shopping malls, or highways. At least these areas tend to have much better infrastructure and security than other locations. Avoid the kind of properties that are adjacent to buildings where crime is known to take place, for example, drug dens and brothels.

## *Misconception 4: Class C Properties Don't Have Appreciation Potential*

As a real estate investor, you understand by now that the biggest attraction to Class C properties is the cash flow rather than the long term appreciation. On the other hand, it would be wrong to assume that all Class C properties will never rise in value. Some areas actually have the potential of being revitalized in the near future, leading to a financial boon for those few investors who acquired property early.

If you buy properties in Class C neighborhoods of large urban areas, it is possible that you may benefit from the path to progress. When an urban area undergoes gentrification, the value of the existing properties within that area may rise. As an investor who is interested in the cash flow of Class C properties, this may prove to be an extra financial incentive. You may be able to sell the property for a higher price than you bought it for.

Of course, it may be difficult to determine whether a city will undergo gentrification in specific areas, but it is still possible to make a smart guess. All it takes is a little research to find out what plans have been put in place in terms of development, revitalization, and renovation. If the upgrading of certain areas is already underway, you will need to move fast. However, there is no need to wait until the last minute. Find out what has been planned by the local authorities and take a calculated risk by purchasing properties in these areas. Even if the gamble doesn't pay off, it will still be a solid financial investment.

You don't have to rely solely on Class A or B properties to generate wealth through equity growth. The value of your property can still appreciate if you buy a Class C property that is located close to or within a Class B neighborhood.

New investors tend to prioritize cash flow over appreciation while more experienced investors often go for a healthy combination of both. A Class C property can put you in that sweet spot. Don't fall for the lie that Class C properties cannot generate equity growth. As long as you have a sustainable investment in a sustainable market, located within the path to progress, you can reap great rewards.

These are the four major misconceptions that real estate investors have to deal with. As you can see, they are all based on assumptions and generalizations rather than facts. Yes, Class C properties have their unique challenges, but so do the other classes of properties. As a savvy investor, always do your due diligence by conducting research about the tenants or neighborhoods you want to invest in. This is how seasoned investors have learned how to turn a profit time and time again.

# Chapter 4: Affordability of Class C Properties

Every real estate investor must determine the affordability of property prior to buying because it will affect profitability and marketability. There are some real estate investors who are of the opinion that the best investments are found in the best neighborhoods, but this is not true. There are good reasons why investors are choosing to acquire properties in lower income areas instead of rushing for the high-end realty market.

Class C properties represent cheap rental units in low-income neighborhoods, and with a massive potential for generating a healthy cash flow. It is safe to say that the affordability of Class C properties is a major factor when it comes to making real estate investment decisions.

So what exactly is it about Class C properties that make them affordable to many investors? Let's look at four specific factors that affect the affordability of these properties:

## *Lower Purchase Prices*

This is the most important reason behind the attractiveness of Class C properties. We all know that they are found in low-income neighborhoods and are usually older buildings that require significant renovations. On the other hand, such properties have really low purchase prices, and when the potential rents are factored in, the return on your investment is impressive.

When it comes to purchasing Class C properties in low-income areas, you may discover that you can get a piece of property for half the price you would pay in a Class A neighborhood. You can then go ahead and charge as little as 15% less in rent. This is a huge opportunity to generate cash flow.

Another way to look at it is to consider how many rental units you can purchase in a Class C area compared to a Class A location. The median price of a single-family home in the Midwest is about $181,000. With this amount of cash, you can buy multiple units in a Class C neighborhood.

These properties are usually sold at double-digit CAP rates, which make them extremely lucrative. It is important to understand what CAP rates are and how they are linked to the overall cost of purchasing a property.

CAP rate stands for Capitalization rate and is a term used to describe the rate of return on properties that generate regular income. It is calculated by dividing your Net Operating Income (NOI) by the purchase price of the property. The

NOI is calculated by subtracting all the operating expenses you will incur from the property (for example, management fees, taxes, and etc) from the annual income you expect from renting out the property.

Let's take the example of a Class C multifamily property. Let's assume that you intend to purchase 12 units at a cost of $500,000, and then charge a rent of $600 per unit per month. Your gross annual income from rent for all the 12 units will be $86,400. Let's assume that the taxes are about $800 per year, and the standard management fees of 10% of the annual gross income to be $8,640. If you subtract the taxes and management fees from the gross yearly income, you get an NOI of $76,960. If we divide this by the purchase price, you get a Cap rate of 15.4.

Property types that have low CAP rates tend to be more stable in terms of asset performance, but they also generate less cash flow. This is where the A and B Class properties fall. They have lower risk potential and higher appreciation compared to Class C properties.

However, as we can see from the example above, a double-digit CAP rate shows you just how good an investment this would be for any investor. When you acquire a Class C property, you buy it at a cheaper price and benefit from the high CAP rate. In order to maintain such a great return on investment, you have to make sure that all your units are occupied and rents are paid on time.

## *Lower Property Taxes*

To be a successful real estate investor, you must be more than just a landlord. You have to think like a smart business executive. By investing in Class C properties, you have the opportunity of leveraging a small cash investment in exchange of owning large holdings that create cash flow and potentially appreciating over time. The whole point of investing in Class C properties is to maximize your profits while keeping expenses low. One of the expenses that you will have to deal with is the property tax.

There are lots of tax advantages to investing in real estate. Class C properties attract very low property taxes compared to the other classes of real estate. You will be required to account for the income you receive and expenses incurred from your rental property, so always make sure that you maintain proper records. One of the expenses that you are allowed to deduct for rental properties on your tax returns is depreciation. Class C buildings are usually old and this depreciation provides you with the opportunity to lower your property tax. Depreciation is a deduction that you claim due to your building wearing out over time. It reduces your taxable income because it is considered an expense, even though money doesn't actually leave your bank account.

As a real estate investor, you also benefit from special tax credits that are provided for investors who acquire and refurbish low-income housing and old buildings. By upgrading these kinds of properties, you gain special tax credits that are a direct deduction from your tax bill. The role of these tax credits is to incentivize investors to put their money into fixing run-down apartment blocks and houses so that these structures do not degrade any further.

It is important to remember that tax considerations should never be the primary motivation for your decisions. Buying rental properties must always be based on the economic benefits. Once you have determined that the investment decision makes economic sense, you should then consider the taxation aspects of the property.

Real estate taxation is an extremely fluid area of the economy, and as such, you should always consult a certified tax professional or advisor who specializes in this field.

## *Lower Maintenance Expenses*

The majority of buildings that are found in Class C areas tend to be in a dilapidated state and require a lot of renovations. This may scare away some real estate investors, but the fact is that you don't have to change much to make the property livable. All you have to do is make sure that there are proper finishes to the property, and these tend to be low grade anyway.

For example, the building may require a paint job. Since it's a Class C property, you don't have to opt for high-grade paints or expensive workmen to get the job done. In fact, if you have the time, you could do some of the painting or other repairs yourself. It is even possible to get the tenants to help in doing some minor repair work in their own units in exchange for some kind of rent deduction. This could be only an annual agreement, and as a result, the property won't drain your financial resources as much.

Most of the people who occupy Class C properties as tenants tend not to be very vocal about major repairs to the building. This is unlike tenants who occupy Class A and B properties. These tenants can be a pain in the neck for any landlord because they complain about everything, even minor or superficial repairs. Class C tenants know that they do not have very many options when it comes to finding other accommodation due to their low-income status.

Of course, just because these types of property require little maintenance doesn't mean you should allow them to fall apart. Remember that your rental units are an investment, so as much as you may benefit from low maintenance costs, you should also consider keeping them in good enough condition to keep the existing tenants happy and also attract new tenants.

When it comes to maintaining a Class C property, do not let the scale of rehabilitation stress you out financially. Most of these kinds of properties are associated with minimal operating costs as part of the primary investing strategy since they are more about generating regular cash flow than appreciation in value.

## *Cash Transactions*

Getting a loan to finance the acquisition of a Class C property can be challenging. This means that investors have to purchase the real estate with their own cash. Fortunately, the purchase price points of Class C properties are relatively low, and this makes it possible to afford them. This would not have been possible if you were planning on buying properties of a higher class, which are obviously more expensive.

One principle that real estate investors live by is this – If it is not worth owning in cash, it is not worth owning. We already talked about how the CAP rate affects the cash flow relative to the value of your property. When evaluating a property, you should also consider the running and maintenance costs, since these will ultimately influence your net operating income (NOI). This generally does not include any loans for buying the property.

By dealing with cash transactions, you end up evaluating a property based on the asset itself rather than the attractiveness of the loan. In other words, just because you get a loan with very low interest rates doesn't mean the property you are buying is worth it. You have to be objective when dealing with Class C properties and view the property on its own merit, and not the strength of the financing.

As an investor, your ultimate goal should always be to own your properties debt-free. With their high CAP rates and low purchase price points, Class C properties are definitely worth acquiring in cash.

The above four factors are all intertwined to make Class C properties more affordable. The lower price points make it easier to purchase in cash, and the lower property taxes and maintenance costs reduce your operating expenses. If you are looking to invest in Class C properties, especially for rental income, you will have to consider each individual building's value based on its return on value. This is covered in the following chapter.

# Chapter 5: Return on Investment for Class C Properties

Every seasoned investor understands just how significant the return on investment (ROI) is when it comes to real estate investing. ROI is a popular and versatile tool that you can use to determine the actual performance of your portfolio. This is especially true for rental properties, since calculating your ROI will help you determine the efficacy of your property.

One of the benefits of investing in Class C properties is a high return on investment. This is down to the fact that Class C properties are acquired at low purchase prices but have the potential of yielding higher rent rates. This makes them high ROI assets.

Determining the actual return on investment for a property can sometimes be a challenge for many investors. This is because the calculation is dependent on certain variables, which in some cases can either be manipulated or excluded from the overall calculation. Determining the ROI of a residential rental property can also be affected by whether the asset was bought on a cash basis or by taking out a mortgage.

## *Calculating ROI*

The return on investment is a measure of the efficiency of an investment. It is an indicator of how lucrative an investment will be and is generally expressed as a ratio or in percentage form. It can also be used to compare the performance of several investments, which comes in handy when you want to find out whether a Class C property would be better than Class A or B. It can also help you know which of your Class C properties will give you a better return on value.

In order to calculate the ROI of your property, the net profit generated by the asset is divided by the amount of money you invested in the asset when buying it.

*ROI = Net Return ÷ Total Amount Invested*

The question we need to ask is how you determine your return on investment for rental properties, and what difference it makes if you buy cash or opt for a mortgage. Let's break this down by looking at a couple of examples:

## 1. Cash transactions

In the last chapter, we discussed the importance and benefits of acquiring your Class C properties on an outright cash basis, that is, without incurring debt. When you buy property through a cash transaction, it becomes much easier to calculate the ROI of the asset.

Let's assume that you bought a rental property for $200,000 in cash at the beginning of the year. You then include other additional costs such as $2,000 for closing costs, and $8,000 for renovations. This brings your overall investment in the property to $210,000.

Let's say that you charge your tenants a rent of $1,600 per month. At the end of the year, you will have collected a total of $19,200 in rent. We need to make this as realistic as possible, so let's deduct two very important expenses that you cannot avoid – property taxes and insurance. Let's take the total expenses for the whole year to be about $3,000. This gives you a yearly return of $16,200.

To determine the ROI of the property, you take the yearly return of $16,200 and divide it by the total investment made of $210,000. This gives you an ROI of 7.7%. This is a very good return.

## 2. Financed transactions

These types of real estate deals make it a bit complicated when calculating ROI. Since we want to compare the two types of transactions and how they affect your ROI, let's use the same amounts as before.

You purchase the same rental property at $200,000 at the start of the year. However, this time you take out a mortgage with a 20% down payment. The down payment will, therefore, cost you $40,000.

You will pay closing costs amounting to $3,000, which is much higher than the cash example because you are now dealing with a mortgage. Let's say that the cost of renovations stays the same at $8,000. The total amount of money invested in acquiring the property will be:

$$\$40,000 + \$3,000 + \$8,000 = \$51,000$$

There will also be ongoing costs linked to the mortgage. Let's say you took a 30-year loan at a 4% interest rate, and the loan you borrowed was $160,000 ($200,000 - $20,000 down payment). In this case, the monthly principal and interest will come to $763.86. For the whole year, this comes to $9,166.32.

It is important to note at this point that calculating your principal and interest on your mortgage is a complex process, and you should use an online calculator to help you out. A good example would be the one at www.bankrate.com/calculators/mortgages.

Next, you consider the cost of taxes and insurance, which we set at $3,000 per year in the previous example. Assuming the tenants pay rent at a rate of $1,600 every month; you will have an annual rental income of $19,200.

Therefore, your yearly return (or annual cash flow) will be:

*$19,200 - $9,166.32 - $3,000 = $7,033.68*

To calculate your ROI, divide the yearly return by the total amount invested (down payment + closing costs + renovation costs):

*ROI = $7,033.68 ÷ $51,000 = 13.79%*

The examples used here are just basic calculations. There are many other extra expenses that affect ROI that an investor incurs when operating a rental property. From the examples above, we can see that the ROI of a financed transaction is greater than a cash transaction. However, there is a bigger picture here that we must focus on.

## The bigger picture

Investors buy Class C rental properties primarily because they want to benefit from a greater annual cash flow. If you look at the two examples, it is clear to see that the cash transaction yields a higher annual cash flow ($16,200) compared to the $7,033.68 from the mortgage deal. This difference is huge!

Another thing to keep in mind is that Class C properties are generally cheaper to acquire than Class A or B properties. If you also consider the rents charged, you will realize that there isn't a big difference between what tenants pay to live in a Class B property compared to a Class C property. This means that the ROI for a Class C property will be way higher than that of either a Class A or B property.

For example, a Class A property may cost you about $800,000 to purchase, with a rent rate of $2,200 a month. A Class B property in the same area may cost $400,000 but with a rent rate of $1,800 per month. Class C properties may cost $200,000 to purchase yet the monthly rental rate can be $1,500.

For a real estate investor, this is great. The purchase price may drop by 50% as you move down a class, but the rent you charge tenants only reduces by a mere 16-18%. The ROI for the properties would be 3.3%, 5.4%, and 9% respectively. The Class C property is a greater value for money hands down!

With such a high ROI and cash flow, you will have enough money to save up and buy another Class C rental property within just a few years. Investing in Class C rental properties gives you the ability to snowball the rents received and acquire similar properties in the long run.

## *Factors to Consider When Buying High ROI Rental Properties*

When it comes to owning rental properties, you have to determine whether it is something that you are willing to do long term. Not every investor makes it in the real estate industry, but if you acquire the right rental property that generates a high ROI, you will be laughing all the way to the bank.

When it comes to considering the factors that affect buying a great Class C property, you have to set your emotions aside so that you don't end up paying too much and regretting the decision later. Here are some of the factors you need to think about:

- **Do your homework** – There is simply no substitute for good education. There may be many investments out there, but they all have one thing in common: If you don't have a clue as to what you are doing, you will get your fingers burned and lose your money! It is important that you first invest in getting a good education. This doesn't mean you have to go to school. You can talk to other more seasoned investors who have a proven track record of making lucrative real estate investments. You can read a variety of books by different authors and determine which strategies work best for you. Avoid the tendency to take investment advice from your broke uncle Charlie, who just watches the news and buys penny stocks. It is amazing how there are so many well-meaning people who are chomping at the bit to give you free advice about things they don't know anything about.

- **Understand your market** – Some of the best Class C properties can be found just within the areas you are already familiar with. This is where you should begin if you are just starting out buying properties. If you aren't familiar with the area, drive around and talk to a couple of neighbors if possible. Chat with local property managers and shopkeepers in order to get a sense of what the area is like and who the potential tenants are.

- **Focus on the income** – As an investor interested in Class C properties, you must make sure that the targeted real estate will generate a realistic and sustainable cash flow every year. Once you have determined your income range, you will then be able to calculate the property's gross annual rental yield as well as its ROI, which you can use to compare with other assets that you want to acquire.

- **Appreciation in property value is secondary** – Class C properties generally produce greater cash flow than appreciation in value. If you look at what happened during the 2008 housing collapse, you will see a trend where investors focused more on the potential appreciation of property rather than generating income. To get a property with a high return on investment, you have to avoid speculating on property appreciation and simply look at the income being generated annually.

- **Don't extrapolate property statistics** – In other words, think local instead of national when looking at statistics regarding property prices. Make sure that the numbers you are looking at are realistic with regard to the local area. The most realistic values can be obtained by looking at the neighboring properties, especially if they have a similar floor plan.

## *Proven Steps for Acquiring High ROI Rental Properties*

1. **Purchase the property at 10-20% below market price** – This will grow your net worth as well as guarantee your financial security. Since you are dealing with Class C properties, which are usually lower in price, you will be able to ensure that you make a great return on investment.

2. **Follow the 1% rule** - Make sure that you set your monthly rent at least 1% of the purchase price of the property. This follows the one percent rule that most real estate investors follow. Some choose to charge a rent of at least two percent of the purchase price to ensure a greater return on investment, especially when factoring in maintenance costs and other expenses. For example, a $100,000 rental property should charge a rent of at least $1000 every month.

3. **Perform due diligence** – Check out the property in advance and determine the scope and scale of repairs that will need to be done. If you have the repair costs and other expenses potentially eating into your rental income and reducing the ROI below 15%, seriously consider moving on to another property.

# Chapter 6: The Risks of Class C Properties

So far we have been recommending Class C properties as a great investment especially for investors who are keen on generating a healthy annual cash flow. The benefits that you have read about are indeed true, but it would be ignorant for you to believe that investing in Class C real estate comes without any risk. We also feel that it is our responsibility to make sure that you understand the risks associated with these kinds of investments.

If you are beginning to consider buying Class C rental properties and becoming a landlord, don't get it twisted. There is no such thing as a risk-free investment. Class C properties are for investors who are willing to take on managed risk with the possibility of reaping higher rewards.

In this chapter, we are going to cover some of the major risks associated with investing in Class C rental properties, as well as their mitigation measures. Risks may be an ever-present component of investing, but as long as you know how to work around them, you will be able to reap good returns.

## *Potentially High Tenant Turnover*

One of the risks that you will have to face is the possibility of a high tenant turnover rate. The fact that you bought the property on the cheap and are charging lower rents than other places does not guarantee that tenants will stick with you for the long term. When investing in Class C properties, you need to understand that getting qualified tenants will not be easy, and you may have to deal with longer vacancies.

The rents may be low but the tenants can be somewhat difficult to deal with, and you may find yourself having to evict some troublemakers on a regular basis. This is normal for Class C properties, and having a high vacancy rate should be something you expect when making that investment. This asset class is said to have an overall vacancy rate of 7.5%.

You can mitigate this risk by having a property manager who is competent and qualified enough to handle issues of a Class C nature. Get someone who knows how to talk to tenants and can stay one step ahead of any issues they may have. A keen and hands-on manager will be able to foresee trouble brewing and start making arrangements in case of random vacancies. Some tenants decide to vacate due to inhospitable conditions, so the solution may be to ensure regular maintenance of critical facilities.

The great thing about Class C properties is that due to the affordable rents, there will be a high likelihood of attracting new tenants even when others leave. All you have to do is make sure that you create an environment within your property where occupants will want to live in. Of course, it won't be the Hilton Hotel, but still, tenants will appreciate it if they see you making the effort.

## *High Crime Rate*

Most properties that are categorized as Class C are usually located in areas where the crime rate is a bit higher than average. The neighborhood may be on the decline and the buildings will be 30 years old or more. The local population is usually lower class, blue collar, and earning hourly wages. These factors tend to exacerbate the potential for criminal activities.

The problem with such a situation is that you may not be able to attract as many tenants as you need to occupy your rental units. At the same time, you may end up harboring criminals within your own building. The issue of investing in a property within a high crime area is one that you simply have to learn to deal with, without passing up great investment opportunities.

So what can you do to mitigate the risk of investing in a crime prone area? You can research the latest crime statistics for the area by going to the website of the local police force. This will give you a clearer picture of what types of crime are common in the area and the frequency and number of incidents per month. Don't assume that all Class C areas have the same level or type of crime. Some places may have high crime but it could be incidents that won't affect your investment property as much. You can also decide to invest in private security for your rental units to keep the criminals away from your property.

The issue of a high crime rate is something that may negatively affect your investment, but once you understand the general statistics for the area, you can take action. If it is a major concern, you could always consider investing in Class C properties that are located in more favorable areas, and avoid the ones that are in very bad neighborhoods.

## *Incompetent Property Managers*

There is nothing as frustrating as having a property manager who is being paid to handle issues and they simply cannot resolve problems. This can be a serious headache if you have invested in a Class C property and your property manager isn't familiar with how such an asset class operates. They may not be comfortable operating a

Class C property, dealing with low-income tenants, or handling issues in a Class C neighborhood. This is a risk that will end up costing you a lot of money.

A property manager should always be someone who knows the lay of the land and can easily interact with the occupants of your property. You will be better off hiring someone who has experience with low-income neighborhoods and isn't afraid of negotiating with such tenants. Remember that tenants in these kinds of areas can be tough to handle at times, so if you have a manager who is uncomfortable taking the heat, get rid of them.

It is important to screen your managers so that you find people who understand how to ensure smooth operation of your property. In fact, spend as much time vetting potential property managers as you do prospective tenants. Get recommendations from other investors who operate Class C properties. You can join real estate investment or property owners associations to get information on who is competent and who isn't.

Interview potential managers in person, if you can, to find out how many units they are managing, whether they own units themselves, and how often they intend to be conducting inspections. These discussions will help you get a feel of whether they are the right fit for your property or not.

Finally, there is one thing that you have to come to grips with as an investor: Nobody will ever manage your property and show more concern for your monthly cash flow than you!

These are the three major risks of investing in Class C properties, but don't let them discourage you. If you happen to be a new real estate investor looking to buy rental houses, then it is recommended that you start with Class C properties. Yes, the risks may be a bit high, but this asset class will provide you with a huge opportunity to make money. If you acquire Class C properties for a low price and maintain or upgrade them, you will be able to elevate them to a Class B and get the right tenants.

Don't believe the naysayers who tell people that there is no money to be made in Class C properties because of the high risk. These are people who are either uninformed or have tainted opinions. What is important is that you understand how to make money off these properties despite the risk factors.

# Chapter 7: Swimming Against the Current

When it comes to investing in anything, especially real estate, you will usually find that most investors follow the herd. Most people wait to see what others are doing and blindly follow their lead without thinking whether that decision is good for their portfolio.

However, smart property investors have learned to go against the grain and practice what is known as contrarian real estate investing. This is where an investor chooses not to follow the masses and decides to do the exact opposite. For example, when you are looking to invest in real estate, the time at which the majority feels euphoric about an investment is usually the point of maximum financial risk. This is the time you should avoid buying property. The time at which the majority feels despondent and depressed about an investment is usually the point of maximum opportunity. This is when you should be lapping up those properties.

Baron Rothschild was a 19th-century tycoon who once said "The time to buy is when there is blood on the streets." In other words, when other investors are running around in a panic, listening to fake media reports, you should be keeping a cool head and buying up that panic. This is the kind of property investor you need to be if you want to succeed with Class C property investments.

There are many factors that influence most investors to avoid Class C properties. These include fear, ignorance (or lack of adequate information), not determining their goals in advance, and failing to evaluate their financial position. Let's take a look at some of the factors that will help you to become a contrarian real estate investor.

### 1. Be Bold

Many real estate investors tend to be afraid of putting their money into Class C properties. They believe that these assets and the communities around them are not a good bet and will not earn them the returns they desire. The majority merely focuses on the high crime, high tenant turnover, and potential maintenance expenses. They allow their fear to blind them to the opportunities within these Class C communities. They make real estate investing an emotional rather than rational decision.

To swim against the current requires a lot of boldness and courage. The majority of investors will tell you that you are crazy, but that is precisely why it is called contrarian investing. Just keep moving forward. Following the herd has, is, and will always be the easiest thing to do. However, if you look at the lives of the greatest real estate investors who have ever lived, you will realize that they all practiced contrarian investing. They simply took bold steps that other people were afraid to take. They didn't listen to the opinions of scared people who were unable to see potential opportunities.

Buying real estate should never be based on emotions and general public euphoria. Success is never an easy road to travel, and you cannot achieve it by blindly copying the masses. This is why only a few real estate investors become wealthy and the majority just gets by. Be bold and don't follow the herd.

### 2. Get Adequate Information

One of the reasons why some investors fear investing in Class C properties is because they don't know anything about these assets. They depend on what they see or hear on the media, and listen to other ignorant people who don't have the right information. The financial media may appear to know everything that is going on, but they rarely give the best investment advice.

These gullible and fearful investors have never been to these Class C areas and end up believing all the negative reports about crime, bad tenants, lack of appreciation potential, and high maintenance expenses. As a result, they follow the masses and opt for higher end rental properties, thinking that they will make more money.

The key to smart investing in any venture is to get the right and relevant information. When you are planning on buying Class C properties, you should do your own due diligence. Visit the neighborhood you plan on investing in and get a feel of the area for yourself. Talk to some of the locals and ask a lot of questions. You can also contact other investors or property managers who own and operate units within such areas. They will help you understand how to handle certain issues and what not to do.

Knowledge is power, and ignorance causes fear. If you take the time to get adequate information in advance, you will be better placed to make your own conclusions. In the world of investing, following the herd is not only foolish but can be costly as well.

### 3. Make a Comparative Advantage

Those investors who avoid Class C properties and opt for higher-end properties have their own reasons for doing so. Of course, there are those who will fail to determine what they intend to achieve and simply swim with the current. Now, there is nothing wrong with investing in Class A and B properties, but what you need to determine is what your goals are. Do you want to buy properties that will appreciate in value over time and earn you a profit, or are you looking for a regular flow of income?

A contrarian real estate investor will always determine what is best for them according to their intended goals. It may not be the popular thing at the time, but who cares? You just need to focus on comparing the advantages of investing in the different asset classes. Obviously, if you want to generate regular cash flow, Class C properties will be the best option. Sure, there are many inherent risks, but that is just part of the game.

Instead of comparing what you have against what other investors are doing, you should perform an analysis of the advantages of Class C properties over the other property classes. As long as the results fit your goals, go ahead and invest, regardless of the direction everyone else is running toward.

## 4. Evaluate Your Financial Position

There are some investors who jump into real estate investing without first evaluating their financial position. If they hear of a hot deal somewhere, they simply go out and get a cheap loan to finance their investments. They end up with a large property portfolio but massive debt to pay back. If the market fails in any way, they will be ruined.

What you need to do is evaluate whether you can actually afford the properties that you want to buy. Keep in mind that Class C properties are generally priced lower than the A and B properties. This means that you have a better chance of buying them in cash. If you cannot afford a property, you may have to get financing as a last resort, but your aim should always be to purchase the real estate free and clear.

# Conclusion

We have now come to the end of the book. We believe that you have learned a lot of great information about investing in Class C properties. Here is a recap of the advantages of Class C properties:

- They are generally more affordable compared to Class A and B properties. They have a lower purchase price, which makes it easier to buy them in cash. The aim should be to own the real estate outright rather than be saddled with long-term debt.

- They have lower property taxes than Class A and B properties. This ultimately minimizes your expenses.

- They require low-grade finishes and have smaller footprints. You will not have to dig too deep into your wallet to perform repairs and maintain the property.

- They have a much higher return on investment compared to Class A and B properties.

- They generate a healthy annual cash flow that can allow you to purchase other lower end properties.

- Due to most tenants being low-income workers, they tend to be lifelong renters who may not be able to afford to move. This minimizes vacancies.

- By investing a bit more in renovations and upgrades, you can elevate your Class C rental property into a Class B, and charge higher rents.

Are you feeling inspired to invest in Class C properties yet? You should! They are a great way to start building your real estate portfolio and generate income. You don't need a lot of money to start, and whatever risks there may be can always be mitigated. All you have to do is make the decision to be bold, educate yourself about property investing, get your goals straight, and evaluate your financial position.

There is never a better time to invest in your future than now. Make that decision today!

Good luck!

www.ingramcontent.com/pod-product-compliance
Lightning Source LLC
Chambersburg PA
CBHW030454220526
45464CB00006B/2542

*9781978150034*